Günter von Hummel

Psychoanalysis / Meditation

Brochure on the Theory and Practice of a new selftherapeutic
Procedure

AF216557

The image on the cover page shows a so-called *formula word* (written on the image of the brain) which is at the centre of the procedure described in this book. It contains different meanings read from different letters of this Latin formulation, a structure that corresponds exactly to that of the unconscious. If one exercises such a *formula word* meditatively and repeatedly, the unconscious must release its own meaning. So in a few lines almost everything worth knowing about this book has been said, which should not prevent you from reading it anyway.

Production and publishing: BoD-Books on Demand, Norderstedt, 2020
ISBN 9783748160373

Table of Contents

I. Theoretical Introduction

Psychoanalysis and meditation are not contradictory. As in one of the usual meditations, the psychoanalyst in his work must also go within himself and abandon himself to the initially unknown darkness as the meditator does.Freud called this an "equal attention", with and from which the therapist should listen to his client. The demand for such a passivity meant that the therapist in this moment cannot (or should not) think rationally and logically. But he is awake, oriented towards the statements of the patient, but still almost in light meditation. For it is important to hear the nuances in the speech of his patients and not the deliberately expressed arguments.

The therapist therefore listens to the completely free, spontaneous flow of speech ("free association") of his patient and has to pay attention to the small fluctuations, stagnations, slips of the tongue, but also to the peculiarities of dreams and fantasies told. In this way he can filter out hidden and repressed meanings, relate them to the therapeutic process and interpret them. Freud his self also expressed himself with regard to "equaly suspended attention" in such a way that the analyst should "turn his unconscious to the patient as a receiving organ".[1] This sounds a little strange. For Freud could not quite clearly define how this kind of virgin conception was to take place, yet interpretations and interpretations are given from the context.

---

[1] Freud, S., G. SW. VIII, S. 381

With the help of meditation all this is easier to understand. In a meditation one lets the spontaneous ideas, the "free associations" of psychoanalysis, pass by more pictorially. One must allow oneself to be "equally attentive", i.e. in the same way as the therapist also handles it in psychoanalysis. But one now waits (with the help of an exercise) until a meaning imposes itself of its own accord, i.e. directly from the unconscious, because it has an - even if not yet complete - interpretation, interpretation.It is entirely up to the structure of the exercise how it comes about that in meditative procedures such interpretations come about from the unconscious. However, the similarities between psychoanalysis and meditation are visible in the form of these two processes (equaly supended attention and free association). In meditative procedures they are usually given other names.

In simple terms, then, one could say that in psychoanalysis the therapist and client meditate together and then interpret the meditated thing together, while the adept who learns a pure meditation does the same with the pure something in front of his inner eye, with the command of his teacher, perhaps with a formula, the process of his breath or something similar.He converses more directly, but also more spartanly with his own unconscious, by putting aside all personal feelings and thoughts. It comes only high in the trance, which strongly pushes him to consciousness and he cannot stop. He converses more directly, but also more spartanly with his own unconscious, by putting aside all personal feelings and thoughts. It comes only high in the trance, which strongly pushes him to consciousness and he cannot stop it. Here, too, thoughts that come in between, trash insights, interrupt the contemplative procedure, just as the excessively free ideas in psychoanalysis also produce a trash of speech. For only a little can be utilized. But also the term 'transference', which is so important in psychoanalysis, plays a comparable role in meditation.

In analytical psychotherapy, feelings and meanings from earlier or current relationships are 'transferred' to the therapist. This 'transference' is unconscious and mostly positive, and the therapist can now give an interpretation of the various relationship events from the aspects 'transferred' to him. He is thus the pivot, the hinge, of the therapeutic dialogue, in short: the actual object, the 'transference'-object, while otherwise subject-related processes take place. In me-ditation, this 'transference' into the darkness, into the nothingness in front of you, takes place inside, and the interpretations must now come directly from the unconscious, and this also from a similar kind of 'transference' object, which I will comment on in detail later.

Of course there are also differences between psychoanalysis and meditation, in the methodical processing, in the further inner procedure, in the meaning of the intellect and other aspects. As much as - as he mentions - the procedure of Analytical Psychocatharsis is easy to learn in practice (only two concentrative exercises are required), it is also necessary to understand and accept the scientific background. A teacher whose personality you believe you can trust and who gives suggestive instructions is no longer enough. Therefore a short theoretical overview.

Already in the earliest human age, when wild, animistic ideas still prevailed, i.e. when it was assumed that everything was equally animated, there were these 'things' on the outside, which were connected to 'things' on the inside, and which interacted and were shaped by patterns of relationships. This interaction between inside and outside was thus formerly dominated by a universal principle of life and has moved mankind since time immemorial and still does today, even if it could never be clearly defined. The matter has not been improved by the modern sciences, also e.g. by something like the science of signs, the semiotics, in which one can connect the signs from inside and outside by identical structures. There is still something indeterminate and blurred about it.

Even in the natural sciences there is the well-known unsharpness-relation, namely that we cannot say anything precise about the smallest units of matter. According to the well-known American physicist L. Randall, we live in a multiverse, whereby the other parts of this multiverse are only 10-31 cm separated from our part.[2] She uses this close connection between macro and micro sizes to describe the connection between quantum mechanics (physics of the very small) and relativity (physics of the very large) within the framework of so-called quantum gravity. But this is not solved and Randall also provides water

---

[2] Randall, L., (Knocking on Heaven's Door) Die Vermessung des Universums, Fischer (2012)

for the mills of all the esotericists who now-more believe that they can explain all the forces that are accessible in and outside of man - such as psychokinesis or clairvoyance. After all, a parallel world, which - because it is insanely close - seems to be almost identical with us, explains every paranormal phenomenon. Quantums intertwine inside and outside, and the soul is nothing more than a quantum-gravitational state of communion inside the human being with the universe outside. This is not scientifically sustainable and thus remains inaccurate.

Similarly, in the humanities, the concept of a universal spirit, the idea of an all-pervading algorithmic information or God,[3] in whose name religious communities wage war against each other because common faith, scripture and theology is not possible for all and thus remains indeterminate. Perhaps it is better from the outset not to start out from the spirit, from algorithmics, from God and not from matter and energy particles, but from units of meaning, i.e. from 'the real (effective) of words and images', which the psychoanalyst J. Lacan called signifiers following linguistics. Although the single signifier is not capable of a specific meaning, only the combination of meanings (signifiers) becomes more and more

---

[3] Harari, Y. N., Homo Deus, Eine Geschichte von Morgen, C. H. Beck-Verlag (2018), in which the author describes that in the future all humans will be controlled only by algorithms. This may well be true, but typically (for today's non-fiction books) there is no indication that there will always be individuals who will see through this and fight against it with the risk of their lives.

real. Thus, framed between two or more signifiers, man reveals himself as a subject to be grasped scientifically.[4] He is then a being caught bet-ween the signifiers, be-tween the 'real word and image', which receives its meaning from the nature of this catchment, and this can be confirmed for psychoanalysis and meditation alike.

Here's the deal: In psychoanalysis neither therapist nor patient knows enough about the other to have a clear picture and be able to make a clear statement. In the therapeutic session, moreover, every usual possibility of communication is lost, there is no topic to talk about, only a free exchange independent of everything. Of course, there is the background of trying to find a common language and there is reason to trust in the science offered. This is also the case in the meditative process of Analytical Psychocatharsis. The node of meaning of the 'real (effective) word and image' is there between the practitioner and the still unclear something, the emptiness, the darkness in front of you. But the meditator is supported by the certainty and security that exists in the formula-words or word-formulas mentioned. For they are already one half of the mentioned transference-object (later further to the other half).

In psychoanalysis as well as in Analytical Psychocatharsis one speaks of two general basic forces, basic drives, basic signifiers, which Freud called for example the Eros

---

[4] 'A signifier represents a subject for another signifier' was one of the sentences most readers of Lacan's works found difficult to understand. The reader of this booklet does not have to deal with this.

life and the death drive. The philosopher I. Kant already began in exactly this sense when he described space and time as a priori, i.e. as given from the beginning as inalienable. And so he saw the first two signifiers, I now call them S1 (signifier 1 for time) and S2 (signifier 2 for space) as determining for man and the world.In this short brochure I stick to this simple, schematic division.

Because more complex representations of these two signifiers often lead to strong abstraction and become impractical. In addition, I can perhaps say that space (i.e. S2) has something to do with the image-real, time (S1) has something to do with the word-real. Because apt words can bridge time or extend it endlessly, while pictures and looks give shape to space, but also imagination. In the end, it will be important to lead both to something in common and yet especially only between them to a successful, more mature and better combination than they usually are.

For the procedure of Analytical Psychocatharsis I will therefore propose two exercises which correspond to these two basic signifiers, S1 and S2, and with which one can also work in fact to find this better combination.Mainly this is the therapeutic help, no matter if you suffer from depressive, anxiety-related or other mental diseases. But the method of Analytical Psychocatharsis is also helpful for those seeking orientation in their life planning, and therefore I will make some academic and theoretical remarks about the nature of the soul and its unconscious forces. It is no longer so much Kant's signifiers, but rather those which Freud called primary drives and meditation teachers mostly called principles, i.e. also primary conditions, which are important for an understanding of the soul.

Derived from perception - I am further oriented here to the French psychoanalyst J. Lacan - there exists (still based on Kant's Spatiality) the perceptual or viewing instinct, to which I assign S2, that which goes from outside to inside. What goes from the inside to the outside, on the other hand, is assigned to the expression or speech instinct, S1, because word-related expression is the most important thing in humans. It is connected with Kant's concept of time, because only since one can say short and boring, timeless, premature and untimely, turn of time and God knows what else, time exists. Time and also the space filled with images and gazes, S1 and S2, are subject-related. In order to give them something object-like, one must do psychoanalysis or meditate.

The meditators now try - if I may continue the game with S1 and S2 - to go back behind the S2, they first switch off the linguistic thinking and expose themselves to the pictorial space. They wait for what emerges from the void from within. It's different in psychoanalysis, where you go back behind the S1. One allows the 'word effect', the verbal signifiers, to become broken units of meaning, to become 'B(r)uchstaben' (a wordplay with broken letters),[5]

---

[5] Oudee Dünkelsbühler, U., Zeugnis und Schrift (Testimony and Scripture): B(r)uchstaben an der Couch, Les Etats Généraux de la Psychanalyse (2001), in which the author means and represents the most elementary intersections and breaks

in order to make them, in a new combination, the definitive statement, the truth of the unconscious and of time. But exactly this never succeeds so exactly. An uncertainty relation remains. I give another example of these processes.

Goethe already wrote: "Two souls dwell, ah, in my breast, one wants to separate from the other". Doesn't this remind you of S1 and S2 ? Doesn't Goethe also want to go back behind this spiritual division in order to be born anew and holistically? For the time being, at any rate, it continues like this with him: "One (perhaps S1) holds on to the world with clinging organs in a crude lust for love; the other (S2) forcefully lifts itself from the dust to the realms of the high ancestors".Even if it is not quite scientifically said, it is the split of the human soul, which reaches deep into the unconscious, almost material, and which is the main subject for psychoanalysis and meditation. For somehow it must be possible to achieve the pleasure with the dust, the linguistic thinking with the pictorial comprehension, in a self-contained soul, in a successful combination. What else should one live for.

In Analytical Psychocatharsis, these two basic forces, drives, which I simply call an Id Rays (S2) and an Id Speaks (S1), are now brought together in a particularly compact and, from the subject's point of view, successful, close combination. For only with such an instrument, which Lacan also called a "linguistic" (Speaks) "crystal"

---

in the psychoanalytic process, i.e. describes a kind of linguistic mathematics.

(Rays), i.e. one that is concise, can work ideally. It's like using a hammer that lies well in the hand, that is easy to grip, which in the method of Analytical Psychocatharsis means: perfectly combined for practical application.Freud already said that the basic drives are always "alloyed", i.e. combined, but in the practice of his therapy they always proved to be bad, combined too contrarily, even almost contradictorily.[6] And so one has to go through a long psychoanalysis. Analytic Psychocatharsis simplifies the process.

Now the comparison between psychoanalysis and meditation and between S1 and S2, can be further improved by looking at the three categories of the imaginary, symbolic and real. They have been introduced by Lacan and are responsible for everything that is at stake. This is especially advantageous for a scientific approach. Thus the theory of the **real** does not convey reality, but the barrier at which one cannot get any further, the obstacles of this world or, as Lacan calls it, the impossible, the invisible 'wall', as M. Haushofer described it in her novel of the same name. Since we no longer bang our heads against reality, because we can change this outwardly real right down to the atom with technology, the psychologi-

---

[6] So also the mentioned Freud's eros-life as well as the death and destruction instinct. But an active instinct directed towards death proved to be impossible. Destructiveness comes from the first modes of identification, where that with which one cannot identify regarding the same object is shifted into negativity and destructiveness. And a combination of the two always leads to something sadomasochistic, which is also not a good starting position.

cally real becomes more of a 'wall' of the inner.It is the point of a constant 'forward failure', of stepping on the spot in an analytical psycho-therapeutic approach.

But also in all meditation methods there is this limit, where one feels that it has reached a strength, which is called mental stability, but which is also often prematurely regarded as the goal, the end of the respective meditation form. Also in meditation one does not become a heavenly stormer, one hardly ever really catches up with what is actually real, unless one is identical with one's doubles (i.e. the S1 and S2), as the philosopher C. Rosset put it.[7] And that's what I want to say actually boils down to, namely the successful, mature, perfect combination of the two. They - S1 and S2, Time and Space, Id Speaks and Id Rays - have of course always been in a certain combination of their own accord, but this combination is uncontrolled, primitive-primitive, not sufficiently good. If it is to become a closed, unified identity, one must improve it and have a key to it.

---

[7] Rosset, C., Das Reale, Traktat über die Idiotie (tract on idiocy), Suhrkamp (1988) pp. 50-63. I am referring here to the state-ment of this philosopher, because he, like Freud, assumes that man is split in himself, and that the real (the psychically real, which also includes the unconscious or neuronal network), which is whole and uniform, only comes to light when one knows his doubles (his shadows, his addictions, his unconscious, his neuronal network) and can completely agree with them, which is probably difficult to achieve in such a direct form. But you have to put it this way.

In psychoanalysis as well as in meditation on the real, it is therefore a last, more or less hardly attainable and - as one has always said - mysterious thing, which one cannot

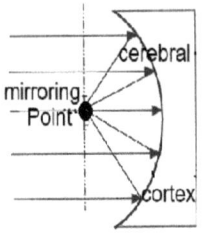 solve further, unless an optimal combination is also achieved in connection with the two other categories, the imaginary and the symbolic. The category of the **imaginary** can be vividly explained from the history of mankind. Thus pre-humans may have perceived the horizon, but they first had to develop the strong temptation to explore the light or lucid that was to be suspected behind it and with each new horizon again behind it.

Curiosity is combined with a seductive shine, with a lucidity that shines through the normal everyday gaze, so that psychoanalysts have spoken here of a second glance, of an unconscious seeing, of a subjective oscillation, an Id Rays, which belongs to the S2. In addition to the usual vanishing point of geometric, perspectival seeing, there is also a reflection point in the centre of the concavity of the brain from which, for example, artists - and especially painters - see the world, but from which the neurotic person as well as the small child can be confused or dazzled.

In meditation, this imaginary is also often called lucidity, a mythical and inner 'light', which is why it is usually recommended to keep the eyes closed when meditating. If one sits in complete darkness long enough, even the colour black starts to glow and causes - as when crossing the horizon - the emergence of another space, another world, the work of the imaginary signifier. This is the subjective gaze, which is also known from psychoanalysis and which interferes with the seemingly objective vision of physiological vision. The philosopher E. Coccia calls it the 'sensual life', the intermediate world of sensuality,[8] which makes us happy and animated. It is boundless and only finds support when the symbolic, the Id Speaks is added. The imaginary, the Id Rays, has the same character and the same value in psychoanalysis and meditation, which is helpful in the transition and cooperation of the signifiers, the 'word-real' (word-effecting) S1 and the 'image-real' (image effecting) S2.

Also the category of the **symbolic**, which I call, analogous to the Rays, also the Id Speaks, can be well explained from the early history of mankind. For the first words were not designations for things or - as many authors think - resulted from gestures. They were rather words of watchwords, words of identity, which were shouted to each other and from which further words developed. The first, seriously emphasized and also repeated several times, tonal, phonetic expression was the starting point of the ultimately verbal language, says Lacan several times in his lectures. And so I can return to God, even if not in this purely denominationally idealized form, as it is still common in religions today, but in the example of the combination of S1 and S2, which is suitable for psychoanalysis and meditation. Also God was an

---

[8] Coccia, E., Sinnenleben (Sensuality-Life), Ed. Akzente Hanser (2020)

identity word, which in the position S2 stood for omnipotence, greatness and beauty but also for anger and wrath, but which, changing into the divine law-giver, is close to S1.

II. Psychoanalysis / Meditation

Back to simpler explanations. As is well known, Freud used to treat people with hypnosis. There, they were immersed in this deeply relaxing, oscillating image, the radiance of their own body image, could 'see' vivid images of early memories and floated as cathartically pleasurable as in a lucid dream. But this cathartic state of happiness was totally dependent on the voice of the therapist, one could only hear his thoughts, so that the people only turned their symptoms into a state of dependency. The images remembered in the hypnosis then - woken up again - did not count for much. Completely in the sense of the 'resistance' against the real uncovering of inner truths known from psychoanalysis, they seemed to be only half hallucinations, to which one did not have to admit oneself.

Freud thus left this method because he wanted the truth to be known to those who were mature from the outset, i.e. who were ready to speak and know. This made it all the more difficult to access the early memories without this unconsciously pictorial, unconsciously imaginary. So he and the psychoanalysts following him had to struggle through endless associations in order to filter out something half-confessed and to put S1 and S2 together to form a truth. The concept of the 'linguistic crystal' for the unconscious introduced by Lacan, however, caused me to reverse the therapeutic procedure. I only had to find the most formal possible way of putting S1 and S2 together and then present this to the unconscious through constant mental repetition.

This word, which I then called the formula-word and which represents the 'linguistic crystal' in the most formal way, could thus burst open the unconscious and give it out in the sense of a truthful way. For the purely formal guarantees neutrality and is at the same time the central pivotal point of the therapeutic event, in which the psychoanalyst also sits in its essential form as an 'object of transference'. As already mentioned in the beginning, the formula word bursts open the unconscious and makes it perceptible, even audible, in thoughts that come from far away. Guarantee for the truthful procedure is the 'linguistically crystalline' way, and the 'transfer-object-like' way in which the formula-word is constructed.

Because by repeating the formula word (or several of them) continuously, one 'transfers' into his nothingness the same positivity as towards a therapist. Previous or other relationships also play a role in this orientation into the dark. While in psychoanalysis the therapist has to dissolve the 'transference' through his interpretations - because the relationships are inadequate, are past or somewhere else current, this dissolving process in meditation is achieved by shifting away such associations in favour of the purely formal exercises oriented and centred on unity, on oneness. So the processes in psychoanalysis and meditation are really parallel and lead to the same results. It is only the focal points that are distributed differently.

Thus one of the main focuses of Analytical Psychocatharsis is the considerably simplified practice. One can practice it at home, the physical presence of the therapist behind the couch, which disturbs many people, and also the dependence on him, which is often problematic, is eliminated. A particular problem in classical psychoanalysis, however, is the therapist's countertransference, which is an automatic reaction to the patient's 'transference'. It expresses itself through emotional, physical and mental events that lead to enactments (constructed interpretations) or mistakes by the therapist, so that Lacan felt compelled to speak of the therapist himself as the greatest resistance to analysis.

As can be seen in the figure opposite-above, the 'linguistically crystalline' tool of Analytic Psychocatharsis is much easier to understand and apply than the psychoanalytic approach.[9] It is the formula-word already mentioned on page two, the Latin phrase which - read clockwise from different letters - contains different meanings. However, the meanings are so disparate that the formulation as a whole cannot be ascribed any meaning. If one practices this writing several times in a row, one's mind

---

[9] For many patients it is difficult to find the words they think they need to say. Nothing is more strenuous than spontaneous, 'free association', i.e. saying everything that comes to mind. Sometimes there are too many ideas, then again one thinks that some of these associations are too superficial.

can't hold on to anything and thus - as already described above - the unconscious is called upon to react to it.

It reacts like the psychoanalyst out of the structure of the 'linguistic crystal' or that of the 'transference' object, as I have already described it as one of the decisive similarities to Analytic Psychocatharsis. This publication, which I also call the Identity- or pass-word, contains the scientifically secured moment of certainty, which replaces the mythical, mystical and magical safeguards otherwise found in meditative procedures, which are no longer contemporary and unscientifically based. For the 'transference' climax, which I have called the cathartic state of happiness from hypnosis, now has a positive, constructive form here and no longer takes place in a relationship of dependence on the voice of the therapist. It has really become the 'object point' of the process.

Only rarely does the psychoanalytic therapist succeed in speaking with the voice of 'nobody' (i.e. the pure 'Id Speaks'), as Lacan demanded, because he must not bring anything personal of himself into play. Formula- and pass-word, on the other hand, convey this voice of 'nobody' much better, more precisely and directly, they only stick to the 'crystalline' structure of the letters and to the linguistic phonemes, the word-sound picture elements. The same applies to the 'empty mirror', which - again according to Lacan - the psychoanalyst should present, in which nothing is already contained (especially nothing from the therapist), so that the patient can see and recognize himself unclouded. This reflection also presents the imaginary, stimulated in the unconscious by the formula-word (unclouded by its non-sense). It presents Coccia's pure 'sensory life', the reflection of the lucid in the concave mirror of the brain, much more effectively than the psychoanalytic situation can ever achieve.

Freud argued that the child is born with a 'poly-morphously perverse' constellation. It behaves - perhaps not so dynamically expressed - completely uncoordinated, made up of impulse pieces, helpless. The student of S. Freud, M. Klein called this initial phase of early childhood 'paranoid/schizoid'. Even if this is somewhat exaggerated, i.e. too psychopathologically formulated, it is, as indicated, a sign of the lack of emotional stability. This 'paranoid/schizoidal' phase or position, which I assign to S2, was contrasted by M. Klein with the 'depressive' phase or position, i.e. position S1, which one reaches after overcoming the first position, because here the mother, the maternal object, e.g. in the form of her breast, comes into play.

The infant is not really depressed, but inhibited, so that he no longer acts out his drives in an extremely uncoordinated and helpless way, but with the help of this maternal object he has grasped a first regularity and can live according to it. Now this first regularity is not the last. I once had an assistant in my medical practice who was a fully qualified lawyer and absolutely wanted to study medicine. Now, after passing the state examination, he said that he could say, from a legal and scientific point of view, that man is a false construction. Is he not a 'half-constriction', I could reply, in respect of which we are called upon to make it whole, well, mature and in a way that is suitable for life'?

So S2 is the first phase or position, which also corresponds to the meditative view, in which one sits down like helplessly facing nothingness and emptiness to begin the exercises. With the first experiences in meditation, however, S1 comes into play here as well, a position that is more orderly, but not yet completely clear, free, successful and good enough, which M. Klein calls inhibited or depressive. In psychoanalysis as well as in meditation, moves of the former position S2 can also break through here, and so one would probably have to get into a position S3, which would be the best solution to the question of the essence of the human soul beyond S1 and S2. Before I give the details of how to perform the procedure of Analytical Psychocatharsis, a brief reference to art, philosophy and science and what they all offer to reach S3.

Freud pointed out several times that art and philosophy always have a certain relation to the neurotic (hysterical), religion and politics to the compulsive, and science (physics, but also psychoanalysis) to the paranoid, delusional. Nothing and nobody can claim absolute objectivity. With the method of Analytical Psychocatharsis, however, I provide something that everyone can try out for themselves in their own practice and thus form their own judgement. The human being, the subject itself, 'Id' in the form of the successful combination of S1 and S2 can achieve a kind of objectivity that is optimal as S3.

As the philosopher H. Hastedt has already described it: "The mind in the participant's perspective, as the subject of cognition, is methodologically superior to mind and body as objects of cognition in the observer's perspective".[10] Once again briefly: The human being as subject being has priority over everything that is called objective by omitting this human core. The actual object, S3, which enables 'transference' and interpretation, is so neutral that one can assign objectivity to it, so to speak, 'the other way around', backwards. Of course, this does not relieve me from following precisely the scientific culture of our time. But it does provide the possibility of a position S3. So now a small scheme to the above mentioned.

The illustration below, which - once again - puts only the all-inclusive comprehensive together in a quite simple and perhaps also curiously formulated way, is intended to provide a general framework, which above all is to be defined and covered by the statements in psychoanalysis by S. Freud and J. Lacan. It has also the advantage that

The imaginary, the pictorial	correlates as art, philosophy	with the hysterical, the neurotic
The symbolic, the worthiness	correlates as religion, politics	with the obessional, the compulsiv
The real, the impossible	correlates as sciences	with the paranoic, the delusional

---

[10] Hastedt, H., Das Leib-Seele Problem (the mind-body problem), Suhrkamp 1989) S. 291

thereby nearly everyone can find himself confronted with something neurotic, to whose clarifying and removal this brochure should serve. I am entitled to say something like that. In the past, it was claimed that man came into the world with an hereditary sin, everyone. Ultimately it is the same thing, we say in this day and age that everyone carries a neurotic conflict within him, which he acquires around his birth, which lurks as division and unconsciousness in the soul's core. The attachments to this are not born to him like hereditary sin, but are given to him very early coming from the most primary intimate relationships, and so it is good to see man from the psychoanalytical perspective like from the outset.

In order to further schematize all this, I place a small picture in the middle of the next page, in which the imaginary corresponds to position S2, the Freudian scopic drive and the essence of elementary 'reflections' (Id *Shines*). On the other hand, the symbolic correlates with the position S1, the speaking drive resp. the 'echoes in the body', as Lacan calls the essence of elementary pronouncements (Id *Speaks*). From my experiences with meditation I have described these groupings with the aforementioned concepts of *Shines* and *Speakes*, because these two basic signifiers or spiritual 'primary objects' are also assigned to the S2 and. S1. It is also about them that one can directly experience in every meditation, by 'seeing' the reflections directly in a lucid form and 'hearing' the echoes in the body just as immediate mentally.

List of opposing terms

Shines	**Speaks**
scopic drive	speaking drive
posit. A, ‚paran.schizoid'	posit. B, ‚depressiv'
the imaginary	the symbolic
mirroring	echoing

The echoes in the body are caused by all the sounds, noises and the daily babble of voices (including that from early childhood) in the body (especially in the brain). There they circle around like unredeemed soul streams in the sense of the earliest repressions. What these echoes are for the symbolic is the so-called ‚primal scene' for the imaginary. According to Freud, it is about the view into the parental bedroom, which confuses the child and excludes it from the intimacy of what is going on there. But the ‚primal scene' can also generally be seen as the completely disturbed imaginary order, where the 'paranoid/schizoid' position dominates. An imaginary order cannot be located as precisely as the linguistic-logical order (M. Klein's second position), which can also explain and include mathematical facts. The images, the seductive but also frightening reflections (S2) simply stand at the beginning. A position S3 is necessary.

The psychoanalysts R. Perelberg introduced the concept of 'Thirdness' in an article, which also deals with position S2 and S1. Thirdness is a third being that not only overcomes the previous position, but also becomes an independent goal.[11] It represents this concretistic fusion of the two above-mentioned fathers' worlds, and also presents the above-mentioned ‚father of the word', the truly symbolic father, as the ultimate goal, in that we can become a part of him. Perelberg shows that already the Oedipus complex marks the significant ‚Thirdness' for psychoanalysis, including the problems of incest, perversion and psychosis, which is in the name of the father, in the symbol of the symbolizing.

However, the ‚Thirdness' goes over and above all these theories, especially through the emphasis on practice, and thus allows us to participate in the symbolic father's practice. So the reader can now gladly forget all that I have written in such a curious and complex way. The philosopher L. Wittgenstein had already said that if one had climbed up the ladder of his philosophy, one should now reject these ladders as nonsensical and continue to see for oneself. No one can tell another what is really effective. However, after throwing away the first leaders, I can offer a second one, which everyone has to tinker with himself, but which in any case will be said to function.

In the process of *Analytical Psychocatharsis*, this happens in the form of thoughts to be heard directly from the unconscious, which I call *Pass-words*, because they ideally reveal the unconscious identity of each individual, so that he cannot obtain confirmation and recognition from anyone other than himself. The *Pass-words* are thus

---

[11] Perelberg, R. J., Murdered Father, Dead Father: Revisiting the Oedipus Complex, Routledge (2015).

words of identification that belong to the respective individual and are not mythical father-words, father references or father complexes that apply equally to all, as those described in Position A and B. They are not the same as the words of the other in Position A and B. They are not the same as the words of the Other. They represent the ,Thirdness', the symbolic father, the position S3.

III. First exercise of Analytic Psychocatharsis

The procedure is very simple from a practical point of view. You sit in a comfortable posture and repeat one, two or up to five *formula words*[12] one after the other in a slow mental process, while at the same time you pay attention to whether something appears that has the character of a Id *Rays*. Only in a second exercise (see later), through concentration of a different kind, an answer (pass-word) to this first exercise is achieved. In the formula words the mentioned "linguistic crystal", the compact combination of the two basic forces S1 and S2 is already pre-realized exactly in the required stringency. It can be used directly in meditation, in psychoanalysis this combination is theoretically well conceived, but not in this practical applicability.

S2, the Rays, which has to do with catharsis, adjusts itself particularly easily, if one looks for something like an inner brightness, a point of lucidity, i.e. something that has the character of a ray, in a comfortable sitting position. It is not about seeing with the eyes, which initially remain better closed, but about something that automatically, a priori (to speak with Kant), just as the S2, the spatial, radiant, appears when one practices for a while. At the same time, the above-mentioned formula words are mentally repeated, which can be created from any

---

[12] Further formula words can be found in other publications or on the website given below. For the time being, the words mentioned here (also in the following) are sufficient. You should not need more than five.

language, but here they come from Latin. In this way, mental repetition and catharsis build each other up. The formula words are purely formal expressions that do not exist in the usual language.

For the formula words I used the Latin language, which is the occidental cultural language par excellence, but which is also particularly suitable for this method. The single formula word is now structured in such a way that it contains several meanings in a single stroke, depending on the letter from which it is read. The formula-word, which also represents a - albeit purely formal - way of speaking, correlates exactly with the structure of the un-conscious, with the B(r)uchstaben, the broken signifiers, 'word effectings'.If one meditates such a formulation several times mentally and also with two or three further formula words, the unconscious is stimulated, even pro-voked, to produce something of its own. What this statement (to give something of one's own) exactly means, I will explain later with the so-called identity or pass-words of the second exercise.

Only in a second exercise (see later), through concentra-tion of a different kind, an answer (pass-word) to this first exercise is achieved. In the formula words the mentioned "linguistic crystal", the compact combination of the two basic forces S1 and S2 is already pre-realized exactly in the required stringency. It can be used directly in medita-tion, in psychoanalysis this combination is theoretically well conceived, but not in this practical applicability.

S2, the Rays, which has to do with catharsis, adjusts itself particularly easily, if one looks for something like an inner brightness, a point of lucidity, i.e. something that has the character of a ray, in a comfortable sitting position. It is not about seeing with the eyes, which initially remain better closed, but about something that automatically, a priori (to speak with Kant), just as the S2, the spatial, radiant, appears when one practices for a while. At the same time, the above-mentioned formula words are mentally repeated, which can be created from any language, but here they come from Latin. In this way, mental repetition and catharsis build each other up. The formula words are purely formal expressions that do not exist in the usual language.

For the formula words I used the Latin language, which is the occidental cultural language par excellence, but which is also particularly suitable for this method. The single formula word is now structured in such a way that it contains several meanings in a single stroke, depending on the letter from which it is read. The formula-word, which also represents a - albeit purely formal - way of speaking, correlates exactly with the structure of the unconscious, with the B(r)uchstaben, the broken signifiers, 'word effectings'.If one meditates such a formulation several times mentally and also with two or three further formula words, the unconscious is stimulated, even provoked, to produce something of its own. What this statement (to give something of one's own) exactly means, I will explain later with the so-called identity or passport words of the second exercise.

First, a German-Latin list of this formula word shown here: The pictorial (imaginary) part lies in the letter images, i.e. only in their pure lines and strokes (where they really are B(r)uchstaben).

The worthy (symbolic) one lies in the different meanings, ideas. One has to see the formulation in a circle, in a line closed to the circle (see figure above), in order to understand the value of this combination of psychoanalysis / meditation correctly. ARE - VID - EOR or ID - EO - R - AR - EV, no matter where you read it from or how you write it, it always has the same character of pure pictograms, but at the same time the character of real words! Through the effect that is achieved in the unconscious, the real also comes into play, and in two different forms: firstly through the catharsis that occurs, which already exists in the meditative process alone and which is not only a psychic liberation but also a 'vegetative switchover'. Secondly, through the change of the conscious and

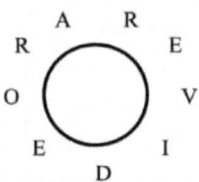

unconscious, when it is forced to the announced release of its contents.

First, a German-Latin list of this formula word shown here: The pictorial (imaginary) part lies in the letter images, i.e. only in their pure lines and strokes (where they really are B(r)uchstaben). The worthy (symbolic) one lies in the different meanings, ideas. One has to see the formulation in a circle, in a line closed to the circle (see figure above), in order to understand the value of this combination of psychoanalysis / meditation correctly. ARE - VID - EOR or ID - EO - R - AR - EV, no matter where you read it from or how you write it, it always has the same character of pure pictograms, but at the same time the character of real words! Through the effect that is achieved in the unconscious, the real also comes into play, and in two different forms: firstly through the catharsis that occurs, which already exists in the meditative process alone and which is not only a psychic liberation but also a 'vegetative switchover'.[13] Secondly, through the change of the conscious and unconscious, when it is forced to the announced release of its contents.

Actually, three or four meanings would suffice for the effect of the *formula words*. Here there are several, many of which seem nonsensical, but this is not a problem. No sense is to be conveyed, and in so far as one or the other listing has a sense, no single, unambiguous statement can be extracted from this single stroke of writing precisely because of the great disparity of all meanings. If too many meanings are conveyed – in psychoanalysis this is called ‚overdetermination‘, in which, for example, many meanings in a dream are condensed into a single dream image – there is no one left for real comprehension. If, however, one remains in the semiwakfulness of meditating, the unconscious itself must give it directly and immediately.[14] It is then a matter of the new sense of posi-

---

[13] I. H. Schulz, the founder of autogenic training, defined this expression for the total state of relaxation.

[14] What Freud calls the 'navel of the dream' has something to do with the original repression, the most original repression or a primary, inner-mental affective anticathexis. In *Analytic Psychocatharsis,* however, this 'Navel' is incorporated into

tion C, which only the immediacy of the unconscious itself can give. So here is the list:

A re videor	I am perceived by the It
Revide ora	Look agaim, speak!
Evide orar	Recognize from it: I am spoken
Vide ora re	Look, speak, in truth!
Vi deorare	Speak with full power
Video rare	I perceive unusually
Ideo rare V	Therefore rarely five
De orare vi	From speaking with persuasiveness
Eo rare vid(E)	Look there seldom!
Arevi deo R.	I am burned by the god R
Orare vide	The praying (speaking) look at!

So even some meanings are not very meaningful - here it's all about the purely structural, the formal. That means the main thing is that on the one hand there are three (or more) completely different meanings in it (in the above mentioned example eleven, which cannot be reduced to any final denominator). On the other hand the lettering as such (precisely because one cannot commit oneself to any meaning if the sequence of letters is written in a circle) is a pure pictorial sequence of letters, a sequence of lines, which has a clear linguistic structure, but says nothing in toto. Thus one follows the psychoanalytical science

---

cognition and self-awareness. It is the interface and break that is produced by the application of the *formula words* and can therefore produce analogous *pass words*. The analogy is 'naive', mathematical, which D. Hofstadter considers in his book ,The Analogy' as scientific proof.

as well as a scientifically founded meditation in the application of such *formula words.*

Nothing works stronger in the unconscious than a sentence that says nothing. Mantra and Koan pof many Asian meditation forms show this clearly. The Chinese hilosopher Zhuangzi taught that one must basically forget everything, the whole culture and everything about it, to the point of confusion. And then he said: 'Oh, if only I knew someone who could forget the language so that I could talk to him! For this reason the client in psychoanalysis should 'freely associate', he should forget the mental-linguistic and only 'babble below himself'. In order to use this fact for Analytical Psychocatharsis, I have developed the formula words, which follow scientific standards and above all Lacanian psychoanalysis, but are suitable for meditation.

If namely three (or more) meanings are united in one word, one coherent formulation, without one of the three (or more) being preferred, then one can, if one repeats this trinity, this triad (as one often says in psychoanalytical jargon) continuously mentally in order to inscribe oneself into that triad, which is the unconscious. So it is already there as a basic complex, basic shape, crystal of the unconscious. Here I repeat some things again, but I also supplement them. Lacan also described the unconscious as "linguistic crystal", and that is exactly what the letter wreath looks like, crystalline (imaginary) and overdetermined ring of letters (symbolic).

The broken-letter-character of the formula word thus becomes visible, and it becomes even more visible, if I introduce this formulation into a geometric form instead of being written in a circle (figure left). In modern Einstein geometry (topology), as is well known, every shape retains its essence even if it is completely deformed, interlaced and twisted. However, interface and fracture points then appear (without the shape really being cut or broken). So I wrote a formula word on a Möbius-band, which has only one surface but two sides (front and back). It is a band that is glued together twisted by 180 degrees, and thus corresponds most vividly to the unconscious, to the splitting of human souls.

This illustration does not serve to complicate my work. The situation is really such that one, if one wants to read in one's own soul, one must adjust to such nested and possibly in broken letters (B(r)uchstaben), which are writ-

ten on topological forms now. Neuroscientists also speak of twisted reflections in the brain. This twist is put back into a straight state with the first exercise of the procedure, in which the crystalline, imaginary, catharsis and lucidity (the *It Shines*) are given a stabilizing direction by the *formula-word* repetition, so that one can then decipher the unconscious text (the *It Speaks)* in the second exercise, as will be described in the next chapter.

As already emphasized, the catharsis of radiance, of the Rays, opens up undreamt-of possibilities. One can have the feeling of being in an hyperspheric space, what mystics used to call the astral plane. But if you stick strictly to repeating the *formula words*, you won't drift away. One then simply remains with the *Rays* as such, with the lucidity of a 'pixelated area', i.e. a point or points of light or reflection, S2. Such a point can appear quite stretched, it topologically does not change its shape as a point (smallest sphere, which can also be topologically deformed). Something else is it, if the brightness itself overflows, then one switches best to the second exercise, the exercise of speaking, the position S2, which will finally lead by itself to S3, to the pass words.

So the Id Rays can be an illumination, a perception of the body, a shimmer, a 'point of light' or anything that has just such a phenomenon. Lacan speaks in this respect of a lucidity, an original 'luminescence'. He clearly refers to something given, something that belongs to the so-called primary process of the drive (here a mental primary object of the viewing drive) and does not have to be artificially striven for. If one wants to represent in relation to an object, this lucidity works like a gaze, the gaze of the unconscious, the radiant gaze, in other words, 'in which one learns to see oneself as God sees one'.[15]

The gaze functions as the primary object of the viewing instinct, but it is a gaze that seems to look at you (in the literal sense) as if from everywhere.In looking, perceiving, seeing, this lucidity is hidden, the Id Rays, an oscilla-

---

[15] Kakar, S., Clement, C., Der Heilige und die Verrückte (the holy and the mad, C. H. Beck (1993) S. 210

tion of looking and being looked at, which was already recognized and described by the philosopher J. P. Sartre. The *Shines* is therefore not something that one has to imagine, create or even force oneself to do. It is present in every human being as the primary form of a force occurrence and must therefore only be awakened or expected. In the same way, however, a 'trickle through', a shivering through,[16] can be felt or the sensation can thaw out, how) own body image shifts, widens, feels like a slight flow throughor it can simply be seen as black paint, a spot in front of the closed eyes.[17] Because black is already a perception, which can rise quite slightly up from the darkness in the head completely small. No matter what is 'seen' or experienced, it will have the character of an so required even very small *It Shines*, and that is enough.

One does not have to attend a course to have this experience, which is authentically present as an aspect of the

---

[16] This is an experience that has something to do with atavistic emotional reactions. Early humans still felt and felt a lot with their uncovered skin and communicated with the environment. Even with moving pieces of music, when it feels like a shiver running down your back, we fall back on these particularly deep emotions. In Analytical Psychocatharsis, this experience is experienced in the form of catharsis, but it is also used as confirmation of an insight, e.g. as a supporting previous experience with the pass words.

[17] All these experiences come from people who have practiced with the procedure or who have developed methods of self-sublimation as in the past in mysticism. In the Old Testament Eliphas also describes the same experiences (Job 4, 12, 15)..

perceptual or visual instinct in every human being. While a slight relaxation has already occurred, this resultis is deepened by the formula words that are repeated at the same time. It is understandable that through the monotonous purely mental repetition of these formulations the *Shines* phenomenon is favoured, which in turn promotes the work of repetition. Both, inner perception of the *Shines* and pure mental repetition of the formula words, are building up.

Again, I would like to mention that this first exercise does not require any effort, especially not to 'see' something with the eye-forehead region! The Rays comes of its own accord, you just have to take care to perceive something that has the c h a r a k t e r of an Id Rays. It can also be the mentioned 'trickling through' that can even mark the catharsis most intensively. Then, at the climax of this experience, one changes to the second exercise, namely, listening to a 'sound', murmuring or thought that has the c h a r a k t e r of an Id Sounds, Id Speaks. Of course you can also set a fixed time of about twenty minutes for each of the two exercises.I will now continue with this.

IV. Second exercise of Analytic Psychocatharsis

In the second exercise, attention is now paid to exactly this *Speaks*, this body echo, i.e. to a sound coming from above or from the right in the head, to a tone, murmur, speech, narration, from deep within. After all, they are letters that emanate from this 'typographic' and hyperspheric space and which the unconscious holds stored there. It is precisely into this space that the formula words have penetrated, awakening and evoking the letters. Again, the same applies here: it is a quite original aspect of the drive to express or speak, the primary object of which is the voice and which is present in every human being as position B, so to speak. It assumes in the unconscious even the form of very brief, compact 'inner sentences', 'ultra-reduced phrases' (Lacan's terms for this phonetic experience). Here, too, at the beginning often only a fine noise, a distant sound or similar can be perceived, but the practitioner will notice from the beginning that this is a concentration on a more above-right or above-central hearing and speech system in the head, to which the echoes in the body have reference, which are used here.[18]

Usually it is the flight of fancy from the first exercise that leads to this second exercise and contributes to the fact that when one concentrates for a longer period of time on

[18] Even if the actual hearing and speech system is placed on the left side of the head, the more rudimentary, musical hearing and speech system on the right side is more accessible to regression and meditation.

the speech, on the unconscious 'sound', the utterance of the pass words will have the effect of being correct (is it not always the catharsis that leads to the fact that even after a sufficiently long time one ends the first exercise and goes on to the second one). The healing power that emanates from the accuracy of the pass words has to do with 'love as a category of knowledge', which also constitutes psychoanalysis. The psychoanalyst G. Kohon calls it 'detached love', which the translator in German expressed with 'separated love'.[19] But it is a detached love, a made-up love, which does not reveal itself, but which at its core is also effective in analytical psychocatharsis, when it is a matter of coming to oneself in a true, mature and successful way.

In Analytic Psychocatharsis one cannot fall victim to a completely absorbing identification with the therapist. Conversely, there is no therapist who has to strive for abstinence and distance but also avoid too much empathy. The 'detached love' that is contained in the entire procedure is sufficient. For this you have to like the formula words from the beginning, because some practitioners have - as already described at the beginning as typical for psychoanalysis - resistance against them.

words, to put it differently with Lacan, are about "a saying as an event, because nothing more than that characterizes love: a flawless saying! A saying "sans bavures", [20]a saying without scratches.This is exactly what the pass

---

[19] Kohon, G., Love in a time of madness. In Green & Kohon: Love and its vicissitudes, Routledge (2005) S. 41 - 100

[20] Lacan, J., Seminaire 21 vom 18. 12. 1973

words do, because behind them there is no ego, no will-fulness, no demand for love and also no sexual desire or gene transfer. This is exactly why the formula words must not say anything definite, this would only cause the everyday unevenness that is stirred up by the usual talk-ing of people among each other and in an unpleasant way. And even more: it is also about saying, which I have already called several times the thought-giving of the unconscious, the hearing, 'listening', of the unconscious thoughts, which represents, apart from catharsis, the ul-timate effect of Analytic Psychocatharsis and which I have called 'pass words' (identity words). Here again I remind you of the compact combination achieved by catharsis and pass words, by the alloy of S1 and S2, which is not made so precise by any other self-therapeutic method. Before I give long explanations, here is another example, which I learned only some time ago from a test person of Analytic Psychokatharsis.

After long meditation, the one who was meditating heard a saying, as if from far away and yet very clearly in him-self, which was called "the deadly loved woman". Loved to death? Sure, clearly, you do not need to interpret it for long. The only question was whether it was your own wife or another one. With his own, it would mean that he would make her life so difficult under a protective pretext of love that one would have to fear death. A. Gide also once described the perfect husband, who could do every-thing, did everything right, and who above all knew how to appear as especially loving without a hint of truth behind it. Gide's protagonist may not have 'loved his wife to death', but he had reified her in a cold and sterile way.The other wife of my proband - and such a lover did indeed exist - was kept completely secret and thus isolated from family and society, in other words a perfectly organized double life, which had 'deathly loving' aspects in the same way, although there was a lot of love here.

In any case, when my test person experienced something like this while practicing Analytical Psychocatharsis, such thoughts about his double life went through his head. Even if they should be negative and one has a resistance against their statement, the pass words show that one is authentic and confronted with truthful self-awareness. One is not so much split into S1 and S2 when one's own unconscious part talks to one, but finds oneself now in the 'third', in S3. One is split when one does not constructively communicate with one's unconscious, but remains rigid and silent. The division as "two opposing and independent attitudes" of the soul is the basis of the psychoanalytical theory of the human person.[21] One remains still and rigid in front of the image in the inner mirror, one does not pass through it, not to the other side of the mirror or the horizon. But if you can hear something from within yourself and find the appropriate interpretation, it is something completely different. Then S3 is reached. My subject began to think in many directions

---

[21] Laplanche, J., Pontalis, J. B., Das Vokabular der Psychoanalyse, suhrkamp wissenschaft (1973) S. 210

and then had extensive conversations with his wives, which brought a solution.

As with the Delphic oracle, but also in many psychoanalytic interpretations and even in religious revelations, the last truth sometimes has to be fathomed a little bit more by additional discussion. It is not difficult to talk to oneself, but not in the form of an ego-monologue, but with the unconscious other within oneself, who is receptive, ready for fertilization and for the birth of truth. The Nobel Prize winner Fr. Handke told a journalist that he often "talks to himself involuntarily".[22] It is probably about exactly the same thing as with pass words, without Handke having made any great comparisons with meditative procedures. With the Other of the unconscious one can make things more authentic, i.e. closer to the real and the truth, which always "involuntarily" comes to light. However, it usually becomes clearer only through additional interpretation and interpretation of what is heard, which does not harm the truth and the involuntariness (which also applies to the real).

In the text I have discussed the more analytical and therefore less cathartic effects of this second exercise. It does not remain with the simple listening and experiencing of inner sound phenomena, but from letter sequences to short sentences. Such short sentences - as mentioned by Lacan also described as 'ultra-reduced phrases' - come directly from the unconscious and thus naturally have to

---

[22] Kümmel, P., Was bedeutet ‚u.‘ ‚S.‘ (What does mean ‚u‘. ‚S‘.) ?, DIE ZEIT vom 2. 12. 2019, S. 44

do with the identity of the practitioner. It is actually about an 'Id tells me', 'Id tells me my own story'. Another example that someone who has been practicing with the method for a long time experienced, I will describe again here.

The person concerned was very interested in religious questions, although he was not attached to any faith or denomination. So while he was busy practicing again for half an hour and just about to finish it, he perceived a thought like "Let's steal the fourth book" rising up deep inside him and almost audible (so his description)! What was that supposed to mean? It soon became clear to him and to me too – since he told me and I knew his religious interest – that it had to be a book of faith, the book that, according to the Old and New Testaments and the Koran, might be another religious book. It is so typical of the unconscious that it had not read: "Let us write the fourth book"! That would have been the typical wish of the committed Orthodox, the full of overly pious wishes of the orthodox, for whom the three great books of faith are not yet sufficient. No, here the unconscious speaks with its characteristic anticathexis, its almost somewhat oracular nature. This fourth book does not exist and it cannot be written. One can actually only steal it!

For it behaves like a stealing when one takes it from one's own unconscious depth. Although it is about one's own unconscious thoughts, they seem strange at first. So you can only steal from yourself. Because, of course, the person concerned is personally meant again. The one who is so interested in religion has to be instructed that none of these faith books has really revealed and will reveal any-thing about religion to him. They can inspire one to con-cern oneself with the religious question. But they will not lead to what those who ultimately wrote these books (or in whose names they were written) were led to back then. The extinct capacity for revelation is well known. My proband also turned to Analytic Psychocatharsis because he was looking for further and different approaches than books, catechisms or preachings zo the psychical, reli-gious, spiritual or whatever one might call it. And thank God he receives the information: in order to come closer to the sacred, you must commit a sacrilege, you must steal from yourself (ek me auton, from myself, as Hera-clitus said).

You can – so the further interpretation, to which my pro-band contributed most – find the truth only on the ways, on which one has already found it before philo-sophically or religiously, namely through a certain paradox. The unconscious does not say (and even a revealing God would not say it today), "read the great books of faith"! No, you must steal away your own ego, your conscious, your ideal ego and ego ideal, your omniscience and your belief in denominations and truncated beliefs. Only the unconscious Other inside yourself is telling the truth. Steal all these pseudo-scientific or other mythical utter-ances circulating in the world. The truth is within your-self and you must find it there and only there. And you have to do it yourself, stealing is a difficult job. It is anal-ysis, but also catharsis. "Let's steal the fourth book" also had a liberating, cathartic effect on the person concerned.

I emphasize again: it is something completely different if the practitioner one day would have had the thought or someone else would have advised him: I should perhaps write something about religion or read another book about it. By this external logic he would have been very weakly convinced. But as this is from deep within, how strange from within it is, the conviction is different. Suddenly out of the 'universal murmur' (the sounds, noises, murmurs, speaking etc.) exactly that *Otherness* of the unconscious itself came out as audible. The Other Himself has spoken.[23] This primarily produces a key-like insight (analytical) and also some psychocatharsis (liberation, cathartic purification). This experience of "fourth book stealing" and the illumination of the meaning behind it has nothing to do with mysticism. It is really about the fact that 'It tells him its own story', 'It, the subject in him, the unconscious, in the language typical of this souls core'.

The fact that these 'inner sentences', these *passwords*, are so concise, 'ultra-reduced' and precise naturally has to do with the same conciseness and precision of the *formula words*. The unconscious is stimulated by such a compact and multi-layered formulation (the meaning of which one has to 'steal') as the *formula words* are to formulate it in the same way. If the combination is really ideal, i.e. if password and catharsis occur at the same time, one can

---

[23] The Other (A, in English O) is an important concept in Lacan's psychoanalysis. Lacan says that the unconscious is the language of the Other within us, in short: it is the *Shines / Speaks* inside us.

also be sure that the statement is correct. Equally important is in addition the rational interpretation of what has been experienced, which, however, usually succeeds without the help of a therapist.

In the state of cathartic switching, it behaves as in the switching of falling asleep and waking up and as in the correct interpretation and revelation in the analysis, namely that an affective climax confirms the source of the affliction and, conversely, that what is true causes an affective climax with revealing insight. So you don't have to be afraid that your ego will be lost if the passwords sound strange. But even if the coincidence of catharsis and password is not so synchronous, the statements – as demonstrated – must be clarified by analytical reflection and questioning. Here a discussion with the therapist can be good if you think you need it.

Everyone must try out here with patience what he can recognize as a password. Sometimes it is the case that one only perceives the short sentence almost in retrospect, in the final phase of the pass-word experience, of listening to the phrase. Sometimes it seems to be a very, very quiet thought, but still clear or quite clear. I have to express myself so diffusely here, yet there is no doubt about the phenomenon, both from the psychoanalytic theory and from the numerous meditative experiences I have been able to collect so far.

As I have already mentioned, one of the main focuses of passwords is that they come over from the unconscious, as if thought by *Another*, as if formulated by an unknown and as if expressed by a knowledgeable suggestion. It is certainly not about God and not only about something repressed, but rather – as the psychoanalyst S. Leikert described it – the creative, the not 'object-relational' uncons-cious, the unconscious rhythmic, comes into play here.[24] In this sense, I want to describe here another and last pass word that I found particularly original. I had a patient who had practiced the method of *Analytical Psychocatharsis* just for a longer period but was also well versed in psychology literature. After she had reiterated a few formula words in a first exercise and perceived a liberating lucidity (*Shines*), she concentrated on the 'sound' (*Speaks*) in a second exercise. As if coming from afar, quietly but clearly she heard after some time of meditation the saying: "Black heard"!

Black heard? Of course, she told me, "you can drive black, exchange black money and hear black, because that's exactly what it is: meditation is not about normal hearing with the ear, nor about hearing with the 'third ear' as the psychoanalyst T. Reik once put it. He said it in a poetically original way, but scientifically one would call it different". I was able to explain it to her again with the term "echoes of the body". I could add that the inner awareness of sounds comes from the 'ultra-reduced phrases' that have to go through the so-called 'narrowings of the signifiers'. These constrictions called by Lacan the

---

[24] Leikert, S., The Kinesthetic Unconscious, Special Issue PSYCHE, Sept./Oct. 2013. This is not about the relationships to fixed psychic 'objects'. Leikert, S., The Kinesthetic Unconscious, Special Issue PSYCHE, Sept./Oct. 2013. This is not about the relationships to fixed psychic 'objects'.

'defiles logiques' are formed by the layers of the hyper-sphere, they are immanent to the signifiers. This hearing that swells out of the 'defiles logiques' is in fact so strange that it can best be described as a 'black hearing'.

My patient also remembered some other things she had more or less 'heard in black': all the intrigues, the mumbo-jumboes, the sentences whispered behind closed doors had been nothing else. One shouldn't have heard them, just as one doesn't want to hear the thoughts and meanings pushed into the unconscious. But what I liked best was the *Password* with the 'black hearing' as essential for meditation. Not always and not everywhere this kind of hearing refers to meditation. The expression is also known for listening to forbidden radio stations during wartime and therefore also fits well for the return of the repressed known in psychoanalysis, now just as an audible return. In *Analytic Psychocathersis* it is the unconscious itself that makes the return audible, in psychoanalytic therapy it has to be done by the therapist together with his patient, where the direct hearing has to be constructed from the associations. As an co-worker, the patient herself will publish her experiences.

V. Conclusions

Let's get back to the exercises: After the first exercise, the mental repetition of several formula words, while simultaneously paying attention to whether one perceives a radiance, a lucidity, a 'trickling', a liberating, cathartic experience, one has transcended body-consciousness (the perception of one's own body image). If the point of lucidity expands into an 'object', into a boundless gaze, a gaze "as God would see you",[25] catharsis is sufficient and then you move on to the second exercise (usually after about twenty minutes). Here one concentrates on the sound, the tone, the speech, from above or from the inner right, until finer tones or even a thought comes up, which can sound like a voice coming from afar, although it comes from one's own body echoes. With the time of the exercises one always gets a clear and secure feeling for the handling of this second exercise (which may last twenty minutes) and the whole procedure.

Since several formula words are needed to practice Analytic Psychocatharsis, I will add two more here. So the following formula word, RA-DIC-IT, which is shown on the cover picture, is not a normal Latin word, but it also contains several overlapping meanings in one formulation, it has a "linguistically crystalline" structure (as mentioned, an expression Lacan uses for the structure of the

---

[25] I quote this sentence of the Indian psychoanalyst S. Kakar again, because it also shows that something critical could be seen, a warning sign, but framed in the positivity of the procedure and thus a meaningful revelation.

unconscious). Apart from radiat and dicit (Rays and Speaks), several different meanings result when written in a circle and read from different letters.So we can also find here, for example, "adi cit r" (approach, it moves

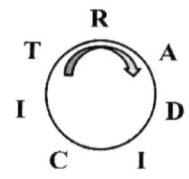

R) "C i tradi" (one hundred i passed), "citra di" (citra di) (the gods on this side), "dicit ra" (it says ra), "r adic it" (add r, it works), "radi cit" (to be scratched, it moves), "trad ici" (tell! I have met) etc., whereby many things sound quite nonsensical. However, this has no meaning for the formal expression. The only thing that matters here is to be able to clearly explain the scientific reasoning (several meanings in one formulation, use of only other interfaces), and this is very important for the procedure, because only then can one have complete confidence in the method.

Once again to the practice: in a comfortable sitting position, with eyes closed or half open, pay attention to the Rays ('Shines', 'trickles', point of lucidity), while at the same time slowly, monotonously and purely mentally repeating one or more formula words one after the other at short intervals and again over again. This is the first exercise that is based on actual guidelines of psychoanalysis, because mental reverberation creates a regression (an inner retreat), which at the same time concentrates only on a narrow aspect of the drive to perceive or look (the Id Rays).

In the same way, formula-word repetition takes the place of what in psychoanalysis is called the compulsion to repeat, the distorted, unconscious repetition. This repetition is difficult to psychoanalyze because it is not represented by psychic 'objects' such as the repressions within, which can be accessed and processed. The psychoanalyst A. Bitsch therefore speaks of the 'good repetition' as it takes place in Analytical Psychocatharsis, in which the unconscious repetition is cancelled by a conscious repetition of the formula words, which also have a distorted meaning, and this once only as long as the exercises of Analytical Psychocatharsis are effective. With the appearance of the pass words, however, the unconscious repetition is finally regulated, just as the correct interpretation in psychoanalysis, once it has grasped the content of the unconscious 'object', cancels the repressions.

After the R-A-D-I-C-I-T, O-R-S-A-C-E-R-A-M can now be added to this first exercise as a further formula word with the following meanings: C eram orsa (a hundred times I was beginning, amor sacer (love is holy), cera morsa (the wax bit), mors acer (death is bitter), amor sacer (love is holy) etc. As emphasized, one can forget these meanings right away. It 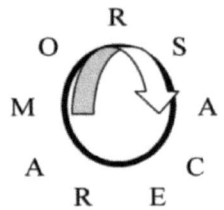 is only important to understand how the formula words are constructed, so that one can scientifically and intellectually question the procedure at any time. If any feelings or ideas come up, which are inappropriate or frightening, one can reflect or read further about the procedure. Blind faith is not required.

The second exercise is even easier to handle. It is about listening to the inside, which will be condensed after a short time in the form of a tone, 'sound', murmuring, whispering up to the hearing of 'ultra-reduced phrases', passages. With time S1 and S2 move more and more together to the closed other of each person, who becomes like a dialogue partner, a communication partner from the unconscious. Already with Lacan many have asked themselves whether his concept of the unconscious other does not concern the same as God. But that is not what it is about, it would only upset the whole field of religion and theology if one would prefer such an interpretation. It is about the unconscious other within yourself, the best friend you can have.

However, the 'trickling' shower of the first exercise of Analytical Psychocatharsis leads one into the second exercise as if floating, which in addition to the relaxing monotony of the formula words also opens the unconscious linguistically. Now the point of the union of the Rays / Speaks as that of the ONE is reached and expresses itself just pass-word for word, from which a confession to the inner truth with a little bit of rational thought aid is easily possible.

If one notices that the ray part is too strong while practicing (or there are too many memories and images), one immediately switches to the speech practice and vice versa (if the inward listening becomes too much coherent). Sometimes other things interfere, such as completely digressive thoughts or somatisation (e.g. chesty cough and the like). Then it is advisable to repeat the formula words very intensively, as if you could think them out loud and with indignation that the right effect does not occur. The compactness of the Rays / Speaks as a successful, close combination, can break through psychosomatic complaints and accelerate the healing process.

The aim of the procedure is to achieve the most ideal, mature, successful and satisfying combination of the two exercises. I cannot give any definite guidelines here, because everyone should be able to know for themselves when S1 and S2, the radiant and the speech exercises, are fulfilling in their combination. After all, experience matures as you progress with the theory, which you can read about or justify yourself further. The alternation between practical experience and theoretical thinking is important because in the end something common will emerge: a mental self-awareness, a practical logic, a cathartic analysis. In the end, both exercises can also lead to an inner 'mission', to a certainty of being able to participate in the shaping of the process as the last-mentioned protagonist did.

Recommendations for further study of literature

Freud, S., Abriss der Psychoanalyse (Outline of Psycho-analysis), Fischer Tb, 1996

Lacan, J., Die vier Grundbegriffe der Psychoanalyse (The Four Basic Concepts of Psychoanalysis), 1980

Weischede, Zwiebel; Neurose und Erleuchtung (Neurosis and Enlightenment), 2009

webpage of the author   >analytic-psychocatharsis.com<

Books published in English by the author

Siri Hustvedt, queer
Literature and an
Advice for Selfanalysis

What about the ONE
The One is only insuffi-
ciently described in mathematics. It is about the
spiritual-physical unity of
man, which can only be
achieved through a combi-
nation of psychoanalytical
and meditative exercises.
The author describes this
process using the literature
of Siri Hustvedt and other
female authors as well as
the psychoanalysis of J.
Lacan.

The physically sick Soul
In booklet of only forty
pages, the author de-
scribes in a simplified
form the method of Ana-
lytic Psychocatharsis that
he developed. It is not
only about the mentally ill
soul, but also about the
treatment of the disorder
expressed in a more phys-
ical form.

The vertical Ego. Just recent psychoanalytical studies have described the very early body-self-mirror-ings, according to which the infant still remains largely in volved in itself. Even in adult life these experi-ences of mirroring the inner vertical, still play an important role. The author shows this with many examples, but also describes a self-therapeutic procedure that is built up from seemingly such contradictory elements as psychoanalysis and meditation.

A Path to self-analytical Practice

Yoga and Psychoanalysis (Language German)

Based on a scientific biog-raphy of the religious scientist and yoga teacher Kirpal Singh (Surat Shand Yoga), all forms of yoga are compared from the perspective of psychoanalysis. It is necessary to establish a procedure of one's own, which the author also calls *Analytic Psychocatharsis*. Numer-ous pictures and diagrams make the book attractive.